# STICKEEN

## John Muir and the Brave Little Dog

by John Muir, as retold by Donnell Rubay
Illustrated by Christopher Canyon

SCHOLASTIC INC.
New York  Toronto  London  Auckland  Sydney
Mexico City  New Delhi  Hong Kong

## DEDICATION

To that lover of stories, my daughter Anastasia. —DR

Dedicated in loving memory to my father, Michael S. Rammell,
and King, our beloved family dog. —CC

ISBN 0-439-08744-9

12 11 10 9 8 7 6 5 4 3 2 1    9/9 0 1 2 3 4/0

Printed in the U.S.A.        14

First Scholastic printing, September 1999

Design by Christopher Canyon
Computer production by Rob Froelick

THIS STORY IS TRUE.

THE GREAT EXPLORER AND ENVIRONMENTALIST, JOHN MUIR, FIRST MET THE LITTLE DOG STICKEEN WHILE EXPLORING IN ALASKA. THIS IS THE STORY OF THEIR MOST MEMORABLE ADVENTURE.

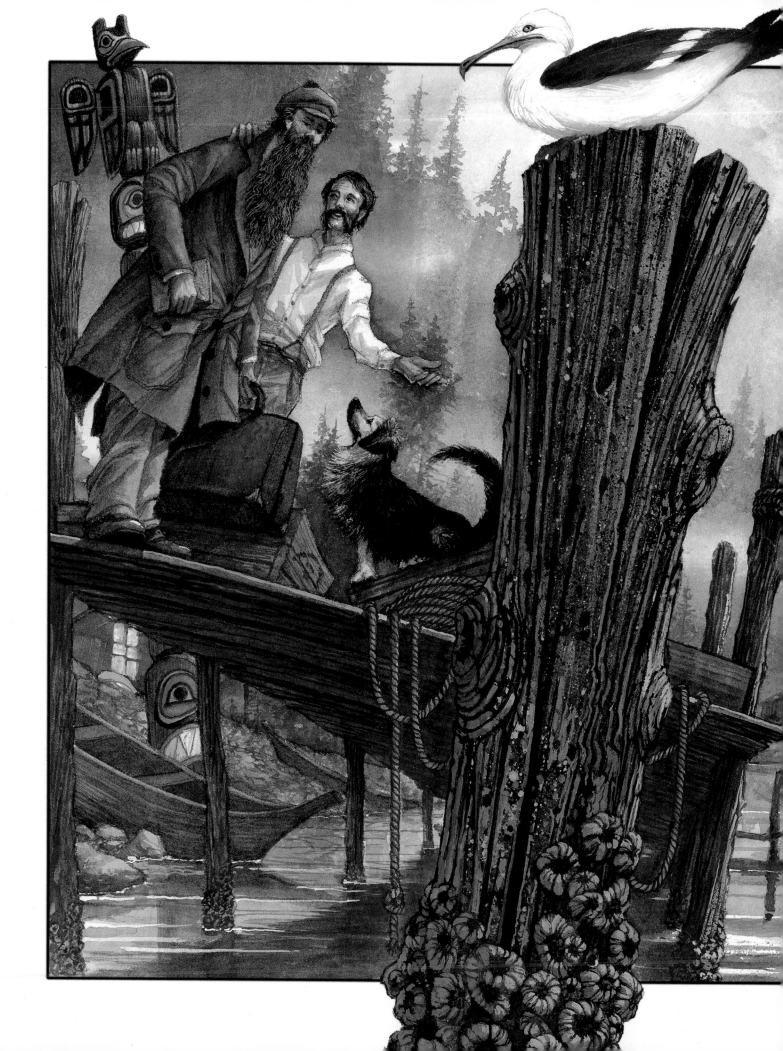

In the summer of 1880 I set out from Fort Wrangel in a canoe. I planned to explore mountains of ice, called glaciers, in Southeastern Alaska. My companions on board included four men and a little black dog. The dog was named Stickeen after the Stickeen Indians. He was a short legged, shaggy pup with a bushy tail like a squirrel's. His dark eyes were sharp and clear.

I did not want to take Stickeen. Before we left I told his master: "Such a little pup will only be in the way. Best to leave him behind."

But his master said, "He will be no trouble at all. He is a perfect wonder of a dog. He can handle cold like a polar bear and can swim like a seal."

As his master spoke, Stickeen looked up at me as if to say: "I am going with you. I will not be left behind."

Our large and sturdy canoe floated down rivers and over waves, past islands and tall cliffs. From the start, Stickeen was a curious character—puzzling and independent. As we rowed, Stickeen spent the days in lazy ease, often seeming to be in a deep sleep. Somehow, though, he always knew what was going on. If a duck or seal attracted our attention, for example, he would rest his chin on the edge of the canoe and calmly look out like a dreamy-eyed tourist. When we talked about making a landing, Stickeen would immediately jump up to see what sort of place we were approaching.

Before we even reached the beach, he leaped overboard and swam ashore. Stickeen was always the first one out of the canoe. Stickeen was also always the last to get in. He could never be found when we were ready to continue our journey. He refused to come when we called. Yet he was watching us from some secret hiding place; for as soon as our canoe set out, he would come trotting down the beach, plunge into the water and swim after us. He knew we would stop rowing and take him in.

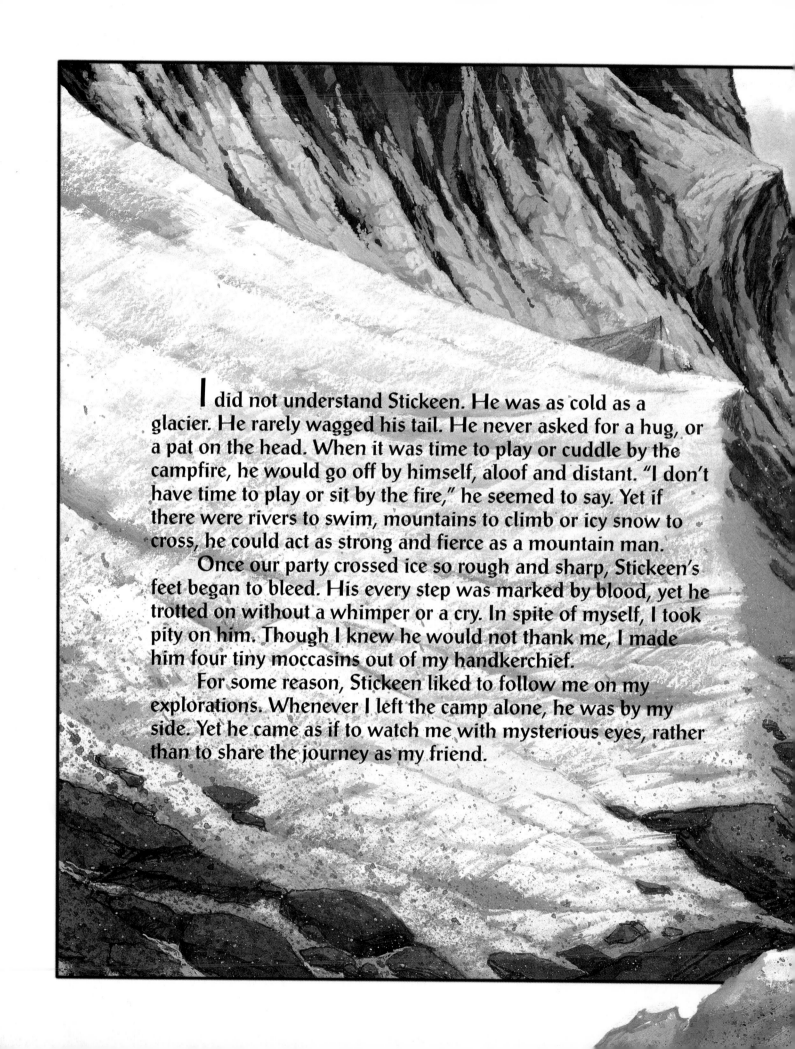

I did not understand Stickeen. He was as cold as a glacier. He rarely wagged his tail. He never asked for a hug, or a pat on the head. When it was time to play or cuddle by the campfire, he would go off by himself, aloof and distant. "I don't have time to play or sit by the fire," he seemed to say. Yet if there were rivers to swim, mountains to climb or icy snow to cross, he could act as strong and fierce as a mountain man.

Once our party crossed ice so rough and sharp, Stickeen's feet began to bleed. His every step was marked by blood, yet he trotted on without a whimper or a cry. In spite of myself, I took pity on him. Though I knew he would not thank me, I made him four tiny moccasins out of my handkerchief.

For some reason, Stickeen liked to follow me on my explorations. Whenever I left the camp alone, he was by my side. Yet he came as if to watch me with mysterious eyes, rather than to share the journey as my friend.

Early one morning, a storm began to blow. Everyone else in the camp was sleeping, but I hurried to explore the music and motion of the storm. Taking my ice-ax, buttoning my coat and putting a notebook and a piece of bread in my pocket, I set out.

I had not gone far when I saw Stickeen running through the snowy storm to join me.

"No, Stickeen!" I shouted at him over the howling wind. "What has got into your queer noodle now? This wild day has nothing for you. Go back to camp and keep warm."

Again and again I ordered him back, but he would not leave. He simply stood in the wind, drenched and blinking, as if to say, "Where you go, I will go."

I could not shake him, no more than the Earth can shake the Moon, so I pushed on. Stickeen trotted at my heels.

All day we climbed the snowy mountains and watched the storm. What a song this storm sang! How fresh the smell of the new snow and the cold, crisp air! When I had the chance, I drew pictures of the white mountains in my notebook. Stickeen stayed a little behind, watching me with secret, distant eyes.

As we continued our journey, we headed toward a large mountain of ice called Taylor Glacier. The glacier rose before us—huge and forbidding—like a great, evil creature guarding a place no man had ever gone.

Many miles we climbed to reach the top of the glacier. There we found a field of ice as thick as a mountain, stretching as far as eyes could see. Eagerly we began exploring.

For a mile or two we found the ice quite safe. Soon, however, we met many long, deep cracks in the ice called crevasses—chasms so deep that no light had ever reached their depths. Death seemed to lie within these holes. Often we were forced to jump these crevasses in order to continue on our way.

One crevasse was so wide that after leaping it, I tottered for several seconds before falling forward to safety. As I rested after this jump I could not help but reflect on how near I had come to death. I have often felt that to meet one's fate on a noble mountain, or in the heart of a crystal glacier, would be a blessed end to an adventurous life. I was sure, too, that I had had happiness enough for a dozen lives. Nevertheless, even the best death, quick and clean, laying so openly before me, was not easy to face.

In contrast, Stickeen appeared untroubled. Though the crevasses lay like bottomless holes before us, Stickeen showed neither caution nor curiosity, wonder nor fear. He sailed over each crevasse like a flying cloud, then trotted on as carelessly as if glaciers were his playground.

Just as day began to fade towards night
and it was time to return to camp, we were stopped by a very large crevasse. Below
my feet, two steep cliffs of ice stretched away from each other. I shook my head.
"This crevasse must be more than fifty feet wide, my boy; far too wide to jump!"
    Stickeen grew quiet. He pawed the icy ground with his foot and
looked up at me with wide, wondering eyes.

Looking for a way to escape, I walked along that deep and wide ice canyon for almost a mile. Could we go back the way we had come? I wondered. No, we had come too far and had crossed many deep crevasses. I recalled the crevasse I had managed to leap, but with no room to spare. I dare not risk jumping it again. Also night was approaching and the sky was dark with the snow of a new storm. Beyond all this, we were wet to the skin and hungry. Were we trapped? Marooned on an island of ice?

Then I saw a thin bridge
of ice stretched across the
crevasse. Fresh snow blew in my
face as I looked closer. I saw that
this ice bridge would not be easy
to cross. It dipped in the middle
like a jump rope held between
two icy giants, and its top was
almost as thin as the blade of a
knife. Also, simply reaching the
bridge would be hard. I would have
to climb about ten feet almost
straight down to reach the nearest
end of the bridge. A similar, almost
straight upward climb waited at the
far end of the bridge. Yet this
frighteningly dangerous route was our
only hope of escape.

Stickeen pressed close to my leg. For the first time, he seemed afraid. He looked at me and began to mutter and whine, saying as plainly as if speaking, "Surely you are not going to try to cross that awful crevasse?"

"Hush your fears, my boy," I said. "We will get across safely, though it is not going to be easy. Often we must risk our lives to save them." But Stickeen ignored my words. He only whined louder and covered his face with his paws.

I took out my ice
ax to chip steps into the
side of the glacier, down to
the ice bridge. Holding on to a
notch in the ice with one hand,
and using the steps I made, I cut
more steps in the ice wall until—
finally!—I reached the ice bridge.

On the bridge I sat astride it, as if
riding a horse. Slowly, I inched my way
across the bridge, cutting off its sharp top
with careful strokes, and creating a narrow
surface about four inches wide for Stickeen to
walk upon. I dared not look down into the deep
blue and white pit plunging beneath me. I kept
my eyes only on the bridge of ice.

Reaching the end of the bridge, I was not yet safe. Almost ten feet of ice rose above me. Weary as I was, I forced myself to focus. I began to chip handholds and footholds into this wall of ice—chipping, climbing, holding on with feet and fingers in mere notches. Never before had I worked so long under deadly strain. How I got up that cliff, I don't know. The thing seemed to have been done by somebody else. A power I could not see or understand had replaced my own small skill and strength!

As soon as I reached safety, Stickeen howled louder than ever. As he howled he ran about searching for another way to escape. "The bridge is not as bad as it looks, Stickeen old boy," I shouted. "You are small enough to walk across."

Stickeen moved closer to the bridge, as if he would try. Then he lay on his back in despair, howling as if to say, "Oh-o-o, what a place! No-o-o! I can never go-o-o across that bridge!"

"If you don't come, Stickeen, I will leave you," I said, pretending to leave by hiding behind a ridge of ice. He did not come.

I went back to the edge of the crevasse and called to him in a stern voice. "I really must go now. I can wait no longer. The storm is growing worse and night is almost upon us."

Stickeen looked at me across that chasm of ice. His eyes were like clear windows into his heart. Though a tiny pup, I saw he was feeling big, wise fears.

I bent to one knee and softened my voice. "If you don't come, my boy, all I can promise is that I will return for you tomorrow. But I can't promise that the wolves, or the coming storm, won't finish you before then."

Stickeen looked around at the growing darkness. He knew I was serious.

At last, with the courage of despair, hunched and breathless, he began to move toward the ice bridge down the ice steps I had made. Stickeen's small body wobbled uncertainly on that almost vertical slope. Steep downward climbs are not easy for dogs.

Stickeen reached the bridge safely. He stood before it and shivered. Snow swirled about him, touching his dark fur and clinging to his whiskers. He looked up at me as he stood at the beginning of the bridge, the deep abyss of ice surrounding him. "I am afraid but I can be brave," I heard him say as clearly as I heard the wind rushing past my ears.

Then, very slowly, he lifted a front paw and carefully took one step. Just as slowly, he lifted a second paw. Another step. Lifting his feet carefully as if counting each step—one, two, three, four—Stickeen walked, ever so cautiously. Longing to help, I kept my eyes upon him, as if they had the power to keep him from falling.

He reached the end of the bridge! But he still had to climb that second, almost straight, slope. Had I a rope, I would have made a lasso to lift him to safety. Yet I had no rope. Stickeen would have to make the climb on his own. Could he do it or would I have to leave him, even though he had come this far?

Stickeen took a long look at the notches I had chiseled in the ice, as if memorizing each one. Dogs are not good climbers. Yet he seemed to know he must not fall now! Carefully he hooked his paws upon a notch I had made.

Then before I could see how he did it, he whizzed to the top—to safety!

"Well done! Well done little boy! Brave boy!" I cried, trying to catch and caress him. But he would not be caught. He darted hither and thither in his great joy, screaming and shouting, swirling round and round in giddy loops and circles like a leaf in a whirlwind, lying down and rolling over, then jumping up to yelp and cry again!

I ran to him to shake him, fearing he might die of joy. He ran off two or three hundred yards, his feet in a mist of motion. Then, turning suddenly, he rushed at my face— almost knocking me down—all the time screeching and shouting as if to say "Saved! Saved! Saved!"

Stickeen seemed ready to celebrate for the rest of the night. Yet we had far to go, and it would soon be dark. I finally persuaded him to continue our journey. On we went, filled with the joy of triumph. Stickeen fairly flew across the snow. Not until dark did he settle into his normal, steady trot.

We reached camp about ten that evening. We found a big fire and a supper that included wild strawberries. But we lay down, too tired to eat much.

Thereafter Stickeen was my true friend. During the rest of the trip he never went off alone. He stayed by my side and always tried to keep me in sight. At night around the campfire, he would come to me. No longer were his eyes mysterious, distant, aloof. He would rest his head on my knee and touch my hand with his tongue. Often he caught my eye and seemed to say: "Weren't we brave, you and I? Weren't we very brave out on that glacier?"

THIS STORY WAS A FAVORITE OF JOHN MUIR'S. He told it many times around campfires and around his dinner table at home. Muir's young daughters, Wanda and Helen, often requested this story. During Muir's lifetime the story of his adventures with Stickeen, particularly the description of the birth of their friendship through adversity, became a classic.

After his explorations in Alaska, John Muir went on to write about environmental issues, to establish the Sierra Club and to help preserve Yosemite as a National Park. Muir received many recognitions for his work. One of these was the creation of Muir Woods National Monument in Northern California.

But what of Stickeen! Shortly after their adventure on Taylor Glacier, Muir and Stickeen explored a second glacier—a glacier later named for Muir. Stickeen's owners, however, were the Rev. S. Hall Young, a missionary and good friend of Muir's, and Mrs. Young. Because Stickeen did not belong to Muir, it was inevitable that the two must part. When this time came, Young was busy saying his farewells and preparing his canoe. Muir, who was to stay behind, settled himself on a coil of rope on the wharf, with Stickeen between his knees.

"Now you must be a brave wee doggie," Muir counseled Stickeen as he had when the two faced the great crevasse on Taylor Glacier. Stickeen wagged his tail, as if to say he understood; yet his despair was great, and clear in his eyes.

Later, someone came to carry Stickeen to the canoe. Painfully, Muir watched as his little friend cried and struggled and reached for him. As Young's canoe rowed away, Muir stood on the wharf gazing after his small partner. Until the canoe passed from sight, Stickeen leaned out of the boat calling to the man who had become both his hero and his friend.

John Muir never saw Stickeen again. Yet he never forgot "the dear little fellow." Nearly thirty years after their adventures, Muir wrote: "I have known many dogs, and many a story I could tell of their wisdom and devotion; but to none do I owe so much as to Stickeen." Through Stickeen "as through a window," Muir saw that love, hope and fear "fall on all alike like sunshine." Therefore, Muir explained, after the adventure with Stickeen, "I have ever since been looking with deeper sympathy into all my fellow mortals."

$J$ohn Muir lived a life filled with adventure and infused with high ideals. Here are some additional sources on this extraordinary man.

**Muir of the Mountains** by William O. Douglas, a young adult biography.

**Stickeen** by John Muir, Muir's second and final published version of the story.

**John Muir, At Home in the Wild** by Katherine S. Talmadge, an 80-page biography.

**John Muir—Wilderness Protector** by Ginger Wadsworth, a young adult biography.

**Son of the Wilderness, The Life of John Muir** by Linnie Marsh Wolfe, a Pulitzer Prize winning biography.

**The Wild Muir, Twenty-two of John Muir's Greatest Adventures** by the Yosemite Association.

John Muir Historic Site

John Muir's deep love for the natural world helped inspire the present-day environmental movement. Millions of people today have a deeper connection with nature as a result of Muir's passionate writings and intense adventures.

Joe Messina

Donnell Rubay discovered the adventure of Muir and Stickeen during a visit to Muir's home in Martinez, California. Believing that today's children would like to meet Muir and his small friend, she retold the story for a modern audience. Rubay formerly taught high school English and Social Studies. Before teaching, she practiced law. She lives in Benicia, California with her husband and daughter.

Jeanette Canyon

In his research for this book, Christopher Canyon traveled much of John Muir's Alaskan route of 1880. Christopher is the illustrator of several children's books, including two published by Dawn Publications: **The Tree in the Ancient Forest**, which won the 1996 Benjamin Franklin Award as best children's picture book of the year, and **Wonderful Nature, Wonderful You.** He also frequently travels to share his enthusiasm for art and nature with children, their families and teachers. Christopher lives with his wife, Jeanette and their cat, Goppy in historic German Village in Columbus, Ohio.